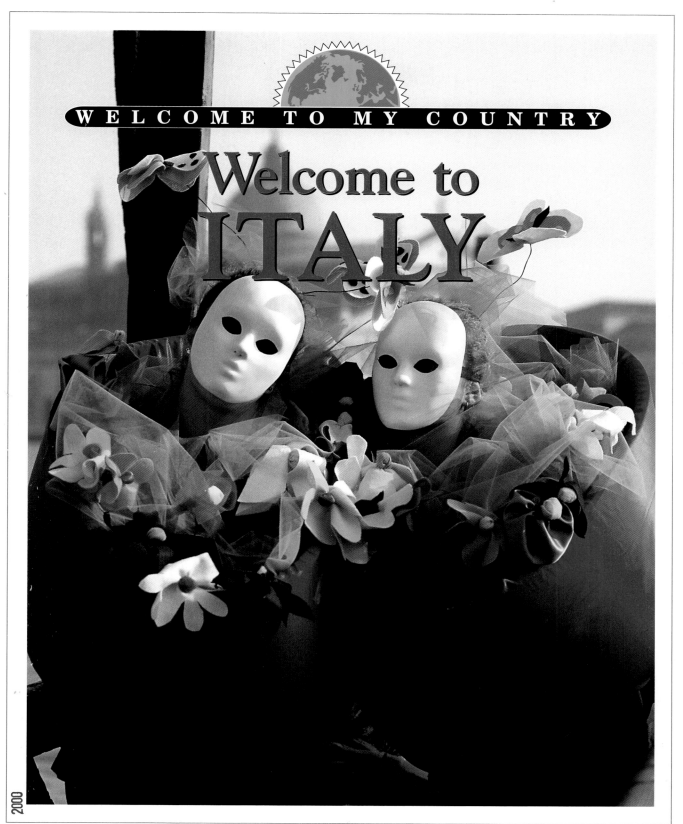

WELCOME TO MY COUNTRY

Welcome to
ITALY

Gareth Stevens Publishing
A WORLD ALMANAC EDUCATION GROUP COMPANY

Written by
NICOLE FRANK/JOSEPHINE SANDER HAUSAM

Designed by
JAILANI BASARI

Picture research by
SUSAN JANE MANUEL

First published in North America in 2000 by
Gareth Stevens Publishing
A World Almanac Education Group Company
1555 North RiverCenter Drive, Suite 201
Milwaukee, Wisconsin 53212 USA

For a free color catalog describing
Gareth Stevens' list of high-quality books
and multimedia programs, call
1-800-542-2595 (USA) or
1-800-461-9120 (CANADA).
Gareth Stevens Publishing's
Fax: (414) 225-0377.

© **TIMES MEDIA PRIVATE LIMITED 2000**
Originated and designed by
Times Editions
an imprint of Times Media Private Limited
Times Centre, 1 New Industrial Road
Singapore 536196
http://www.timesone.com.sg/te

Library of Congress Cataloging-in-Publication Data

Frank, Nicole.
Welcome to Italy / Nicole Frank and Josephine Sander Hausam.
p. cm. — (Welcome to my country)
Includes bibliographical references and index.
Summary: An overview of the geography, history, government,
economy, people, and culture of Italy.
ISBN 0-8368-2510-1 (lib. bdg.)
1. Italy—Juvenile literature. [1. Italy.] I. Hausam, Josephine Sander.
II. Title. III. Series.
DG417.F73   2000
945—dc21   99-089188

Printed in Malaysia

1 2 3 4 5 6 7 8 9 04 03 02 01 00

PICTURE CREDITS
Giulio Andreini: 3 (bottom), 5, 9 (bottom),
   22, 43
Bes Stock: 3 (center), 4, 11 (top), 12
Camera Press Ltd.: 15 (bottom), 29 (top)
Paolo Ciucci: 9 (top)
Focus Team Italy: 3 (top), 7, 40
Haga Library Inc., Japan: 1, 2, 8, 20, 21, 24,
   26, 28 (left), 29 (bottom), 38, 39, 41, 45
HBL Network Photo Agency: 23, 28 (right), 30
   (both), 33
Ingrid Horstman: 27
The Hutchison Library: 19
Illustrated London News Picture Library: 13,
   15 (center)
Sheila McKinnon: 10
North Wind Picture Archives: 11 (bottom),
   15 (top)
Topham Picturepoint: 14, 16, 17, 18, 32
Trip Photographic Library: Cover, 6, 25, 31,
   34, 35, 36, 37

Digital Scanning by Superskill Graphics Pte Ltd

Contents

Words that appear in the glossary are printed in **boldface** type the first time they occur in the text.

Welcome to Italy!

Italy played an influential role in Western civilization for hundreds of years. Today, Italy is a country where old and new combine to form a unique and interesting culture. Let's take a closer look at Italy, a country of contrasts, where beauty and function, prosperity and poverty coexist.

Opposite: Gondolas wait for tourists across from the impressive church of Santa Maria della Salute in Venice.

Below: An artist carefully works to restore a painting damaged by time and pollution.

The Flag of Italy

Italy's flag, the Tricolore, has three panels of green, white, and red. It was adopted by a few Italian city-states in 1797, when French Emperor Napoleon Bonaparte controlled the region. In 1861, it became the flag of the Kingdom of Italy.

The Land

Into the Sea

Italy is the fourth largest country in Western Europe, with a land area of 116,333 square miles (301,302 square kilometers), including its small islands.

The Italian coast, which stretches about 5,000 miles (8,045 km), faces four seas — the Ligurian, Tyrrhenian, Adriatic, and Ionian. Each is a branch of the Mediterranean Sea.

Below: The snow-covered Dolomites in the northeast attract many skiers during winter.

Peaks and Valleys

Mountains cut across Italy. In the north, the Alps form a natural border between Italy and central Europe. Mont Blanc, the country's highest peak, is part of the Alps and reaches 15,771 feet (4,807 meters). The Apennines extend down the center of Italy.

The Po Valley, in the north, is Italy's largest plain. The Po River flows into the valley. The Arno, Tiber, and Volturno are other major rivers.

Above: The Egadi Islands, with their beautiful beaches and clear, blue water, are a favorite tourist stop.

Seasons

Despite its sunny reputation, Italy has unstable weather. The position of the sea and mountains leads to changes in temperature and rainfall. Each region has a unique climate.

Left: Monte Cervino lies between Italy and Switzerland. Also known as the Matterhorn, it reaches a height of 14,690 feet (4,478 m).

The Alps have long, harsh winters and short, cool summers, while the Po Valley experiences snowy winters and humid summers. The Apennines get heavy rain all year except during summer, and Italy's western coast receives rain year round. The southern coast of Italy is dry, warm, and sunny.

Plants and Animals

Trees cover about one-fifth of Italy. Oak, beech, fir, and pine trees grow in the mountains. Poplar and willow trees grow in the Po Valley, while cypress and umbrella pines thrive in central Italy. Olive trees dot hillsides throughout the country.

Except for the wild boars in Sardinia, few other wild animals remain in Italy. Chamois (small antelope), foxes, ibex (a kind of goat), black bears, and wolves reside in remote mountain areas.

Above: Conservation projects over the last twenty years have helped raise the number of wolves from 100 in 1970 to about 500 today. Italy's wolf population lives in national parks and nature reserves.

Left: Italy is one of the largest producers of olive oil in the world. The most productive olive orchards in Italy are located in the southern regions of Calabria and Apulia.

History

Early Settlers

Over six thousand years ago, early European hunters crossed the Alps and entered Italy. They formed tribal groups and spread across the country.

Around 800 B.C., the Etruscans, who probably came from an eastern Mediterranean country, arrived in Italy. Skilled in art, metal crafts, and sports, the Etruscans strongly influenced the Roman people.

Below: The Greeks first came to Italy around the eighth century B.C. Sicily is home to some of the most beautiful Greek temple ruins in Italy, many of which can be found in Temple Valley in Agrigento.

The Roman Empire

Etruscan rule ended in 510 B.C., and Rome became a republic (a government with representatives). The republic ended in 49 B.C., when Roman general Julius Caesar took power. A two-hundred-year period of peace, called the Pax Romana, began in 29 B.C.

Below: Ancient Rome was a civilized society, where people led **lavish** lifestyles.

In A.D. 476, the Roman Empire collapsed. Charlemagne, who was crowned Holy Roman Emperor in 800 A.D., briefly united northern and central Italy. This unity ended when he died.

Fighting for Unity

From the eleventh century, city-states ruled Italy and prospered during the **Renaissance**. Many European nations, however, wanted to rule Italy, and the country was invaded often. After invasions by France, Spain, and Austria, Italy was divided.

In 1833, a secret society began working for national unity and independence. France joined Italy to fight the Austrian army in the north. In 1861, northern and southern Italy were united. Ten years later, Rome was made the Italian capital.

Below: The Vittorio Emanuele II Monument in Rome is a symbol of Italian unification.

Left: Benito Mussolini (*front row, second from left*) ruled Italy for nearly twenty years under a form of strict, **authoritarian** government called fascism. He is seen here with German leader Adolf Hitler (*front row, second from right*).

The World Wars and Mussolini

After an initial pledge of **neutrality** in World War I, Italy supported the Allies. Although the Allies won, Italy had large war debts and lost 350,000 men.

In 1919, Benito Mussolini led a movement, called **fascism**, to protest the war. He became prime minister of Italy in 1922 and **dictator** in 1925.

Italy and Germany joined forces in World War II. Many Italian lives were lost in the war. Mussolini was voted out of office in 1943 and executed in 1945.

The Birth of Democracy

In 1946, Italy became a republic. In 1948, a new constitution was adopted, and rights that were taken away by the fascists were given back to the Italians.

Italy became a member of the North Atlantic Treaty Organization (NATO) in 1949 and a member of the United Nations in 1955. Italy was also a founding member of the European Economic Community, called the European Community today. Italy remains a democracy to this day.

Below: Italian Prime Minister Romano Prodi *(back row, fourth from right),* U.S. President Bill Clinton *(front row, fourth from left),* and other world leaders met at the 1997 NATO Summit in Madrid, Spain.

Julius Caesar (100 – 44 B.C.)

Julius Caesar conquered England and Germany during the period of the Roman Republic. He took power in 49 B.C., declaring himself "Emperor for Life." He was killed on March 15 in 44 B.C.

Julius Caesar

Giuseppe Garibaldi (1807–1882)

In 1848, after becoming a war hero in Uruguay, Giuseppe Garibaldi returned to Italy to help fight the Austrians. With the help of a volunteer force, he conquered Sicily in 1860. He died a national hero.

Giuseppe Garibaldi

Benito Mussolini (1883–1945)

Benito Mussolini led the fascists in 1919. He was named prime minister in 1922, after he and his followers threatened violence on Rome. In 1925, he became a dictator, calling himself *Il Duce* (il DOO-chay), or "the leader." He ruled until 1943.

Benito Mussolini

Government and the Economy

Government

Over fifty governments have ruled Italy since World War II. Most were in power for less than a year.

The Italian Parliament has two houses — the Chamber of Deputies and the Senate. Parliament members serve for five years. The Parliament elects the president who serves for seven years. The president appoints a prime minister.

Left: Romano Prodi, Italy's former prime minister, was elected to Parliament in 1996.

The prime minister and cabinet members have no fixed time in office but can be voted out by the Parliament.

Although the Christian Democrats have dominated post-war politics, there are two other major political parties in Italy — the Democratic Party and the Socialist Party. At least nine other parties are active in each election. Over 85 percent of Italians vote.

Above: Political rallies are held in the streets during election years.

The Economy

Italy is one of Europe's richest countries. Its main economic sectors are tourism, manufacturing, and agriculture. Italy has a high gross national product (the total value of a country's goods and services in a year), but it still has economic

Below: Oranges and other citrus fruits are important agricultural products.

problems — high unemployment rates in the south, high social spending, and inefficient government-run companies.

Grains, sugar beets, olives, grapes, and tomatoes are Italy's principal crops. Orchards of cherries and apricots thrive in southern Italy.

Italians raise cattle for their meat and milk. Tuna, shrimp, octopus, and squid are all fished from Italian waters.

A million tons of marble are cut from the Alps each year. The town of Carrara is the marble capital of the world.

Cars, computers, and chemicals are all produced in the areas around Milan, Turin, and Genoa. Italian clothes and fashions are known around the world. Iron and steel, appliances, and processed foods are other successful Italian industries.

People and Lifestyle

Settling In

Italy's first inhabitants arrived over six thousand years ago from Russia and central Europe. Later, the Greeks and the Phoenicians from the Middle East established communities in Italy.

The Etruscans, Germans, and Arabs, as well as the Normans and Gauls from France, have settled in Italy. Spaniards and Austrians also influenced Italian

Left: Italy's population is a mix of many of the major cultures in the world.

culture because their countries at one time ruled different sections of Italy. Italy's unique cultural background has resulted in a complex ethnic **heritage**.

Regional Differences

Italy is divided into regions, some of which are isolated because of the mountainous countryside. Italians take pride in the traditions of their particular regions.

Living, the Italian Way

About a third of Italians live in cities, such as Rome and Naples. Very few live on the slopes of the Alps and the Apennines. Today, many people are moving out of the city to the less expensive and quieter **suburbs**.

Most people live in modern apartments or old houses. Italians typically have neat, clean homes.

Left: Visiting the city square is a popular family activity on Sundays.

Above: Shoppers inspect produce at the unique Venetian floating market.

The *salotto* (sah-LOH-toh) is a formal room in the home where families read, watch television, and entertain guests. People eat in a room called the *sala da pranzo* (SAH-lah dah PRAHN-zoh). Most homes have balconies that provide useful extra space for plants and hanging laundry.

Most Italians buy meat, fruit, and vegetables at small, local markets. Large cities have special streets lined with expensive and elegant shops, One such street is the Via Condotti in Rome.

Education

The Italian school year runs from September to mid-June. Children attend school six days a week, from 8:30 a.m. to 1:30 p.m.

Students have nearly three months of summer vacation, when most children do "vacation homework" to review the year's school work.

After five years of primary school, which starts at age six, students take an examination to enter middle school.

Left: It's play time at school. Many children under six years old attend kindergarten.

At fourteen, students attend one of three types of secondary schools. The *liceo* (lee-CHAY-oh) offers classes in the arts, languages, and sciences. Technical institutes offer **vocational** courses. The *magistrale* (mah-gee-STRAH-lay) is for future teachers.

Students take a nationwide exam to enter a university. Over 1.2 million students attend Italy's universities.

Left: A priest celebrates Christmas Mass from the ornate altar in the Church of Santa Croce in Florence.

Religion

About 95 percent of Italians are Roman Catholic. The spiritual and governmental center of the Roman Catholic Church is Vatican City, a city-state in Rome.

Many Catholics in southern Italy also follow folk beliefs. Protestants, Jews, and Muslims worship in small groups throughout Italy.

Roman Catholic History

In A.D. 33, Roman governor Pontius Pilate ordered the execution of Jesus. Three centuries later, Christianity was accepted and legalized in Rome.

In A.D. 324, Roman ruler Constantine built a church over the tomb of Jesus's apostle Peter. It has since been rebuilt and named the Basilica of St. Peter. Today, this church is the center of Vatican City.

Left: John Paul II became pope in 1978. He has absolute authority in the Catholic Church and rules over Vatican City.

Language

Official Italian

There was no common national spoken language in Italy until 1870, after the country was united. One dialect, spoken in Florence during the 1300s and 1400s, was chosen as the basis of modern Italian.

It took another hundred years for "official" Italian to flourish. Today, it is used in schools and on television and radio. The roots of the Italian language come from Latin, which is still used in some Catholic churches.

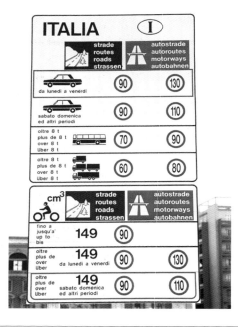

Far left: Most Italian road signs are written in Italian, French, English, and German.

Left: Dante's *Divina comedia (The Divine Comedy)* describes the poet's journey through hell, **purgatory**, and heaven. It is one of the greatest literary works of all time.

Dialects

Many Italian dialects, regional words, accents, and pronunciations evolved from Latin and other ancient Italian languages. In some areas of Italy, only local dialects are spoken. Today, dialects are written down and recorded in order to preserve Italy's past.

German, French, Croatian, Greek, and Albanian are spoken in Italian border areas.

Above: Umberto Eco's first novel, *Il Nome della Rosa* (*The Name of the Rose*), was an international bestseller. It was made into a film in 1986.

A Well-Written Story

Dante Alighieri, author of *The Divine Comedy*, is Italy's greatest poet. His epic poem is one of the most influential Italian literary works of all time. Other classical Italian writers include Horace, Ovid, and Virgil.

Niccolo Machiavelli, Baldassare Castiglione, Luigi Pirandello, and Italo Calvino have all made their mark on Italian literature. Italian playwright Luigi Pirandello won the Nobel Prize for Literature in 1934.

Below: This sculpture depicts Italian writer Carlo Collodi's classic children's story, *Pinocchio,* about a puppet that comes to life.

Arts

The Renaissance

Art has always played an important role in Italian life. Even buildings have been decorated to depict religious beliefs and stories.

From the 1300s to the 1500s, Italy was the center of an artistic explosion called the Renaissance, meaning "rebirth." Much of this art was created for the church. Botticelli, Bernini, Michelangelo, and Titian were brilliant artists from this period.

Above: The distinctive portraits by modern painter Amedeo Modigliani are world famous.

Left: The Renaissance period saw the rise of talented painter and architect Raphael. One of his most famous works is the **fresco** entitled *School of Athens.*

Italian Architecture

Italian art is visible in buildings throughout the country. Some baths, theaters, temples, and public buildings from over two thousand years ago are still standing. Cathedrals, such as the Duomo of Orvieto, which took three centuries to build, are examples of great Italian architecture.

During the Renaissance, classic Greek and Roman designs were reintroduced. A good example of this architecture is St. Peter's Basilica in Rome. The architecture of Florence also flourished during this period.

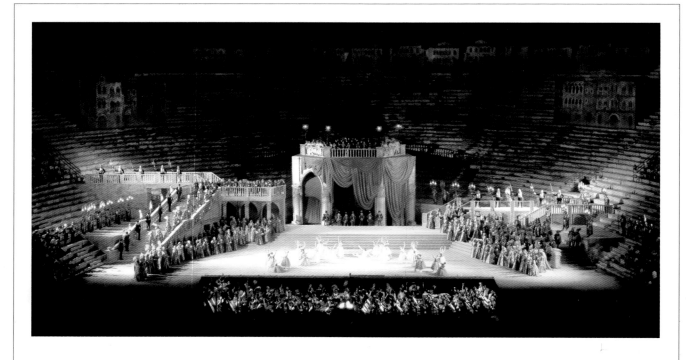

Music and Opera

Italians have made vast contributions to the world of music. Madrigals (a form of poetry and music), opera, orchestral music, and musical instruments such as the piano, cello, and violin are all Italian creations.

Italians love opera. Many famous operas, such as *Madame Butterfly* and *Aida*, were written by Italians. Giuseppe Verdi and Giacomo Puccini are well-known Italian operatic composers. Renowned Italian opera singers include Enrico Caruso and Luciano Pavarotti.

Above: The opera *La gioconda* (*The Joyful Girl*) was composed by an Italian, Amilcare Ponchielli, in 1876.

The Italian Film Industry

After World War II, directors started making films about everyday life in Italy. Roberto Rossellini, Vittorio De Sica, and Federico Fellini are famous Italian directors. In 1999, Italian director/actor Roberto Benigni won several Oscars at the Academy Awards ceremony for his film *Life is Beautiful*.

Left: Italian actress Sophia Loren delights audiences around the world. In 1961, she won an Academy Award for her role in the Italian film *La ciociara* (*Two Women*).

Leisure

Italians have a reputation for being lively, warm, friendly, noisy, and outgoing. Their spirited words, expressions, and gestures fill conversations with excitement. In Italy, hugs, kisses, and handholding are very common between friends.

Cafés, restaurants, and private homes are all popular spots for social gatherings. Every town has a *piazza* (pe-AH-tsah), or open square, where people gather to chat, shop, or play

Below: Everyone goes to the piazza to play, shop, or chat at cafés. It is always bustling with people and activity.

cards. Italians also spend leisure time taking a *passeggiata* (pah-seh-jee-AH-tah), or walk.

Time to Relax

Much of Italy rests in August, when people head to resorts for vacations. Most Italians stay in Italy for the holidays, although, lately, an increasing number travel to other countries.

Many Italians enjoy going to the opera, watching television, and reading newspapers and magazines during their free time.

Sports

Soccer is the most popular sport in Italy. Both professionals and amateurs play the sport, which is followed closely by devoted spectators. Every Sunday, soccer stadiums are packed with fans eager to see the action.

Italians of all ages enjoy cycling, skiing, golf, car racing, and tennis. Bocce, a game played on a dirt court with a set of wooden balls, is a distinctly Italian pastime.

Left: Cyclists race through the streets of Italy every May in the Tour of Italy bicycle race.

Staying Active

Cyclists fill the roads during Italy's many bicycle races. The cycling world's premiere event is the Tour of Italy, which attracts the world's best cyclists. Over a three-week period, competitors ride from Sicily to Milan.

Italian slopes are the perfect spot for skiers to test their skills. Water sports, such as sailing, swimming, diving, and fishing, are also very popular.

Above: The Mille Miglia is one of the world's toughest auto races. The race covers 1,000 miles (1,609 km) of Italy's public highways.

Left: Colorful carnivals take place throughout Italy in final celebrations before Lent. Giant floats and costumed people crowd the streets. Excited onlookers line the carnival route.

Festivals and Holidays

Historical and cultural festivals liven up cities across Italy throughout the year. Each year, Verona hosts a Shakespeare Festival. Venice is the site of an annual international film festival.

Food is honored in many festivals, such as the Fair of Mutton Chops in Castel San Pietro and the Festival of Spaghetti in Torre Annunziata. In wine regions, the grape harvest is celebrated.

Christmas is one of the most important religious festivals in Italy. Mass is held at midnight on Christmas Eve. Children go from church to church to see the beautiful nativity scenes.

Left: The most important event in Italy is Holy Week. Processions with marching bands and people in colorful costumes take place in many areas of the country.

Food

The art of cooking thrives in Italy. Pizza, pasta, ***prosciutto*** (proh-SHOO-toh), ***cannoli*** (kah-NOH-lee), ***gelato*** (jeh-LAH-toh), and ***cappuccino*** (kah-pooh-CHEE-noh) are all Italian specialties. Italy has borrowed food and recipes from around the world, making their dishes mouthwatering and unique.

Each Italian region has its own specialties. Naples is famous for pizza, Sicily for sweets, Tuscany for soups, and Lombardy for rice dishes.

Left: Pasta has been part of the Italian diet for hundreds of years. Spaghetti is the most popular form of pasta.

Italian Meals

Breakfasts in Italy tend to be light, with the main meal served at noon or in the evening. Meals usually begin with *antipasti* (ahn-tee-PAHS-tee), or a plate of appetizers, followed by soup, often a thick vegetable soup called *minestrone* (mee-neh-STROH-nay). Pasta, served with tomato, cheese, or *pesto* (PEH-stoh) sauce, is the next course. In the north, *risotto* (ree-SOH-toh), a rice dish, is served instead of pasta. Meat, vegetables, salad, and fruit complete the meal.

	A	B	C	D

SWITZERLAND

AUSTRIA

HUNGARY

TRENTINO-ALTO ADIGE

Monte Cervino
(14,690 ft /4,478 m)

Mont Blanc
(15,771 ft /
4807 m)

VALLE D'AOSTA

FRIULI-VENEZIA GIULIA

SLOVENIA

1

FRANCE

Turin

Milan

LOMBARDY

Verona

VENETO

Venice

CROATIA

PIEDMONT

Po

Po Valley

Po

LIGURIA

Genoa

EMILIA-ROMAGNA

Bologna

Castel San Pietro

BOSNIA HERZEGOVINA

MONACO

Carrara

Pisa

Arno

Florence

A D R I A T I C

2

LIGURIAN SEA

TUSCANY

MARCHE

UMBRIA

Orvieto

S E A

VATICAN CITY

Tiber

ROME

ABRUZZI

LATIUM

MOLISE

Volturno

APULIA (PUGLIA)

3

SARDINIA

Mount Vesuvius
(4,190 ft/1,277 m)

Naples
Torre Annunziata

BASILICATA

CAMPANIA

TYRRHENIAN SEA

CALABRIA

N

IONIAN SEA

4

M E D I T E R R A N E A N

Egadi
Islands

Mount Etna
(11,053 ft/3,369 m)

SICILY

Agrigento

S E A

5

ALGERIA

TUNISIA

MALTA

	State Boundary
■	Capital
●	City
	River

ITALY

42

Abruzzi C2
Adriatic Sea C2–D3
Agrigento C4
Algeria A5
Alps A1–C1
Apennines B1–C3
Apulia (Puglia) C3
Arno River B2
Austria C1

Basilicata C3
Blanc, Mont A1
Bologna B2
Bosnia Herzegovina
    D2

Calabria C4–D4
Campania C3
Carrara B2
Castel San Pietro B2
Cervino, Monte A1
Croatia C1–D1

Dolomites B1

Egadi Islands B4
Emilia-Romagna
    B1–B2
Etna, Mount C4

Florence B2
France A1
Friuli-Venezia Giulia
    B1–C1

Genoa A2

Hungary D1

Ionian Sea D4

Latium B3–C3
Liguria A1–A2
Ligurian Sea A2
Lombardy B1

Above: Parade participants take a well-deserved pizza break.

Malta C5
Marche C2
Mediterranean Sea
    A4–C5
Milan A1
Molise C3
Monaco A2

Naples C3

Orvieto B2

Piedmont A1
Pisa B2
Po River A1–B1
Po Valley B1
Puglia C3

Rome B3

Sardinia A3

Sicily C4
Slovenia C1
Switzerland A1

Tiber River B2–B3
Torre Annunziata C3
Trentino-Alto Adige
    B1
Tunisia A5
Turin A1
Tuscany B2

Tyrrhenian Sea B3–B4

Umbria B2

Valle d'Aosta A1
Vatican City B3
Veneto B1
Venice B1
Verona B1
Vesuvius, Mount C3
Volturno River C3

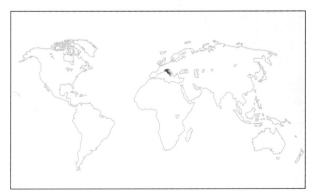

Quick Facts

Official Name	Republic of Italy (Repubblica Italiana)
Capital	Rome
Official Language	Italian
Population	58,138,000
Land Area	116,333 square miles (301,302 square km)
Regions	Abruzzi, Apulia (Puglia), Basilicata, Calabria, Campania, Emilia-Romagna, Friuli-Venezia Giulia, Latium, Liguria, Lombardy, Marche, Molise, Piedmont, Sardinia, Sicily, Trentino-Alto Adige, Tuscany, Umbria, Valle d'Aosta, Veneto
Highest Point	Mont Blanc (15,771 feet/4,807 m)
Longest River	Po River (416 miles/670 km)
Major Mountains	Alps, Apennines, and Dolomites (part of the Alpine range); volcanoes include Mount Etna and Mount Vesuvius
Major Religion	Roman Catholicism (95 percent)
Currency	Italian lira (1,986 lire = U.S. $1 in 2000)

Opposite: The Leaning Tower of Pisa is one of the most famous landmarks in Italy.

Glossary

antipasti (ahn-tee-PAHS-tee): appetizers.

authoritarian: related to a government or leader that enforces absolute obedience to authority.

cannoli (kah-NOH-lee): pastry that is shaped like tubes, deep fried, and filled with cheese and other ingredients.

cappuccino (kah-pooh-CHEE-noh): coffee with steamed milk.

dictator: a ruler with absolute power and authority.

fascism: a political system in which the government, the economy, and society are controlled by a dictator, who is usually supported by a strong army.

fresco: a picture painted on a plaster wall when the plaster is still wet.

gelato (jeh-LAH-toh): Italian ice cream.

heritage: culture and traditions passed down from ancestors.

lavish: abundant and extravagant.

liceo (lee-CHAY-oh): academic school.

magistrale (mah-gee-STRAH-lay): a school for teachers.

minestrone (mee-neh-STROH-nay): thick vegetable soup.

neutrality: the position of a country not to participate or take sides in a war between other countries.

passeggiata (pah-seh-jee-AH-tah): a walk or stroll.

pesto (PEH-stoh): a sauce made from olive oil, herbs, and pine nuts.

piazza (pee-AH-tsah): an open, park-like place in a city.

prosciutto (proh-SHOO-toh): spicy Italian ham.

purgatory: according to the Catholic Church, a place where the souls of people who have died are prepared for eternal life in heaven.

Renaissance: the period between 1400 and 1600 when classical ideals of art, literature, and learning were revived in Italy and the rest of Europe.

risotto (ree-SOH-toh): rice.

sala da pranzo (SAH-lah dah PRAHN-zoh): a small dining room.

salotto (sah-LOH-toh): living room.

suburbs: residential areas on the outskirts of a town or city.

vocational: related to education and training focusing on skills needed for a particular occupation.

More Books to Read

Daily Life in Ancient and Modern Rome. Cities through Time series. Joan D. Barghusen (Lerner Publications)

The History of Emigration from Italy. Origins series. Katherine Prior (Franklin Watts)

Italian Renaissance. Living History series. John D. Clare, editor (Gulliver Books)

Italy. Festivals of the World series. Elizabeth Berg (Gareth Stevens)

Italy. Major World Nations series. Kathryn Bonomi (Chelsea House)

Michelangelo and the Renaissance. Great Artists series. David Spence and Tessa Krailing (Barrons Educational Series)

Pompeii: The Day a City Was Buried. Christopher Rice (DK Publishing)

Rome. Cities of the World series. Richard Conrad Stein (Children's Press)

Videos

Italy. (Madacy Entertainment)

Italy: Pizza, Pasta and Panache. (Tapeworm)

Italy: Rome, Vatican and Galleries. (Education 2000)

Italy: Venice, Florence. (Questar Inc.)

Web Sites

touritaly.org

www.odci.gov/cia/publications/ factbook/it.html

www.Italyemb.org

www.supersurf.com/italy/

Due to the dynamic nature of the Internet, some web sites stay current longer than others. To find additional web sites about Italy, use a reliable search engine and enter one or more of the following keywords: *Julius Caesar, Italy, Mediterranean, Benito Mussolini, pasta, pizza, Renaissance, Rome, soccer, Vatican City, Venice.*

Index